African and Asian Dance

Andrew Solway

Heinemann Library
Chicago, Illinois

Customer Service 888-454-2279
Visit our website at www.heinemannlibrary.com

Editorial: Sarah Shannon and Robyn Hardyman
Design: Steve Mead and Geoff Ward
Picture Research: Melissa Allison and Hannah Taylor
Production: Duncan Gilbert

Originated by Modern Age
Printed and bound by Leo Paper Group

13 12 11 10
10 9 8 7 6 5 4 3 2

Library of Congress Cataloging-in-Publication Data

Solway, Andrew.
  African and Asian dance / Andrew Solway.
    p. cm. -- (Dance)
  Includes bibliographical references and index.
  ISBN 978-1-4329-1379-3 (hc)
  1. Dance--Africa. 2. Dance--Asia. I. Title.
  GV1751.S55 2008
  784.18'8--dc22
                          2008014297

Acknowledgments
The publishers would like to thank the following for permission to reproduce photographs:
© africanpictures.net p. **8** (Independent Contributors/Guy Stubbs); © Alamy Images pp. **12** (Maciej Dakowicz: www.pbase.com/maciekda), **13** (Paul Doyle). ©Redferns/Pankaj Shah, **23** (Dennis Cox), **31** (John Eccles); © Corbis pp. **5** (Reuters/Yuriko Nakao), **6** (dpa/Rolf Haid), **9** (Keren Su), **14** (epa/Kerim Okten), **18**, **26**, **32** (Lindsay Hebberd), **25** (Caroline Penn), **28**, **41** (Robbie Jack), **33** (Charles & Josette Lenars), **34** (Reuters), **42** (Reuters/China Photos); © Getty Images pp. **4** (The Image Bank/Eric Meola), **10**, **19** (The Image Bank), **15** (AFP); ©Redferns p.**21** (Pankaj Shah); © Still Pictures pp. **16** (C. Jacques Jangoux), **22** (Joerg Boethling), **36** (Das Fotoarchiv/C. Achim Pohl); © The Kobal Collection pp. **29** (Golden Harvest), **37** (Yash Raj Films); ©Topfoto p. **39** (A©National Pictures).

Cover photograph of an Intore dancer from Rwanda, reproduced with permission of © Lonely Planet Images/Ariadne Van Zandbergen.

Every effort has been made to contact copyright holders of any material reproduced in this book. Any omissions will be rectified in subsequent printings if notice is given to the publishers.

Disclaimer
All the Internet addresses (URLs) given in this book were valid at time of going to press. However, due to the dynamic nature of the Internet, some addresses may have changed, or sites may have changed or ceased to exist since publication. While the author and publishers regret any inconvenience this may cause readers, no responsibility for any such changes can be accepted by either the author or the publishers. It is recommended that adults supervise children on the Internet.

Contents

Drumbeats and Rosebuds...................................4

A Dance for Every Occasion.......................8

Temples and Courts...............................12

Music and Dance.................................16

Styles and Techniques.........................20

Telling Stories...............................24

Masks, Costumes, and Makeup...............30

Spreading the Influence.....................34

Changing Styles............................38

The Dances of Africa and Asia.................44

Glossary.......................................46

Further Information.............................47

Index...48

Some words are printed in bold, **like this**. You can find out what they mean by looking in the glossary, on page 46.

Drumbeats and Rosebuds

A group of dancers moves together in a line. Their feet make quick stamps on the floor in time with a rapid drumbeat. Their backs ripple to the rhythm of their feet. With arm and body gestures, they emphasize another drumbeat in the music, playing a different rhythm. Then the music changes, there is a flurry of movement, and one dancer breaks from the line to do a **solo**.

▼ In Mali, western Africa, Dogon dancers wear masks and costumes during funeral and death ceremonies.

▲ Kabuki is a traditional Japanese form of movement and drama. In Kabuki, the female parts are played by highly trained male actors called *onnegata*.

In another dance, a single figure appears on stage, moving with small, gliding steps. The dancer's face is white except for a mouth painted like a red rosebud. The dancer wears a white **kimono** and carries an umbrella. The dancer's body ripples like liquid from one pose to another. The music is a song about a heron that was once a beautiful woman. The dancer's movements and the singing create an atmosphere of sadness and regret.

These are two examples of the dances of Africa and Asia. The first is a festival dance from western Africa. The second is the start of a Japanese Kabuki play. Asia and Africa are the two biggest continents in the world. There is a huge variety of dance across these vast expanses of land. However, we can divide Africa and Asia up into a few large regions, each with its own dance styles and history.

Dance facts

Dancing in your street
Even if you have never seen any African or Asian dance, you have probably seen dance with African or Asian connections. Jazz dance, hip hop, salsa, samba, and many other dance styles from North and South America are related to the dances of slaves from western Africa. And the dancing in Bollywood movies (from India) has strong connections with two styles of Indian dancing.

Dance regions

South of the Sahara desert, the dance and the music of Africa have many things in common. Rhythm is important in both music and dance from this region. Often, several different rhythms run through the music. Dancers pick up on these rhythms through complicated step patterns or by moving their legs to one rhythm and the rest of their bodies to another.

Dance and music north of the Sahara have strong connections with the Middle East. Most countries in north Africa and the Middle East follow the religion called **Islam**. Dance and theater are not particularly important arts in Islamic countries, but there are many kinds of **folk dance** and some religious dances.

India, Pakistan, Bangladesh, Sri Lanka, Bhutan, and Nepal together make up South Asia. The region has a long history. In the past, all of South Asia was ruled as one kingdom. Dances were important parts of court entertainment. They were also one way of worshiping the gods. Although different parts of South Asia have different kinds of dance, many of them are connected through these ancient court and temple dances.

Southeast Asia includes Burma, Thailand, Malaysia, and Indonesia. The region is rich in dances. As in India, there are traditional court

The Cloud Gate Theater of Taiwan combines modern dance **choreography** with movement from traditional Chinese forms, such as Tai Chi and Chinese Opera.

and temple dances that are very old. The traditional court dances are related to those of South Asia, but there are also hundreds of other kinds of dance. China, Japan, and Korea are the main countries of East Asia.

China and Japan have their own dance-drama styles that are different from those of South or Southeast Asia.

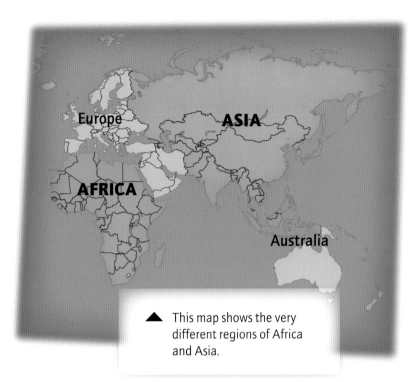

▲ This map shows the very different regions of Africa and Asia.

Dance connections

Dances from western Africa may seem very different from those of Asia, but we can find connections between them. For example, rhythm is an important part of both Indian and African dances. In many African dances, a solo dancer has a "conversation" with the master drummer or lead musician, where the master drummer plays a short phrase then the dancer responds using movement. Something similar happens in sections of Indian kathak dance, where a dancer will begin by either stamping out or sometimes speaking a rhythm. The musicians then pick up the rhythm and play it back to the dancer, who follows on with another rhythm.

From traditional to modern

Many of the dances of Africa and Asia are traditional, which means that they have a long history. This book will look at why traditional dances were originally danced and how they have changed over the years. But it will also cover recent dancers and choreographers (people who create dances) who have helped to bring African and Asian dance into the 21st century.

Amazing fact

War dances
Another connection between African and Asian dance is the war dance. In South Africa, young Zulu and Ndebele men learn athletic war dances that celebrate past battles of their tribes. Baris is a traditional war dance from Bali, Indonesia, that is now performed as a temple dance and for tourists. Beijing Opera is a dance, theater, and music spectacular that has been performed in China for hundreds of years. In the battle scenes, large groups of dancers perform amazing feats of acrobatics and martial arts.

A Dance for Every Occasion

Have you seen an African dance performance? You may have seen one in a theater or at a festival of some kind. However, traditional African dances were not made for performing on stage. Each dance was made for a particular occasion.

Past and present

In the past, music and dancing were a part of life in Africa. On any occasion when people got together, there was music and dancing. There were dances when a baby was born or to celebrate the **"coming of age"** of a young adult. Even when a person died, there were dances at the funeral ceremony.

In recent times, more and more African people have moved into cities, away from the families and communities where they were born. They no longer learn the dances for particular occasions. But music and dancing is still important in African cities. Most people dance for fun in dance halls and clubs. Some new kinds of dancing have developed. Gumboot dancing is a kind of competitive dance that developed in South African mining areas in the 1970s. Large groups of miners from many different areas lived together in organized housing. They got together in groups and formed dance teams, which competed with each other. The dancers wear gumboots (rubber boots), which they slap and stamp as part of the dancing.

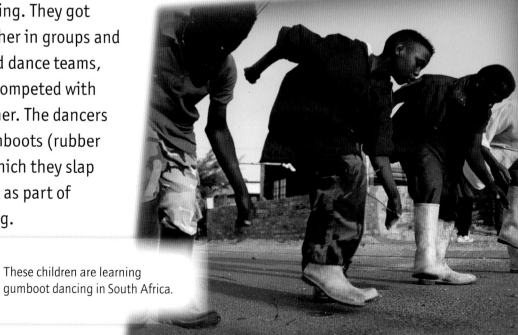

▶ These children are learning gumboot dancing in South Africa.

At the age of 15 or so, Maasai boys become *morani* (warriors). In the warrior dance, they compete to see who can jump the highest.

Occasions for dancing

Many traditional African dances are related to work. Hunting dances mimic the movements of animals or of the hunter shooting an arrow. Fishing dances mimic movements such as rowing and casting nets. Other dances might represent workers pounding or grinding cereals to make flour or building a new house.

Other traditional dances mark special occasions in people's lives. Many African societies have ceremonies for young people's "coming of age." When Maasai boys from Kenya reach the age of about 15, they shave part of their hair, dye it red with **ocher**, and become *morani*, or warriors. The *morani* live outside the village and perform special songs and dances together. In the songs each *moran* boasts about his skill at hunting, and in the dancing he tries to jump higher than all the others.

Funerals of important people are another major occasion for dancing. There are also ceremonies to remember **ancestors** and leaders who have died. The funeral dances of the Dogon people in Mali are spectacular events that have become famous, attracting visitors to the area.

In African societies where there are kings or chiefs, some dances are made for royal occasions. When a Yoruba king is crowned, he leads a dance procession through the streets, followed by his family and other followers. Other dances and celebrations are related to religious worship. In Africa today, most people are either **Muslim** or Christian, but this was not true in the past. Many African people believed in gods and spirits that could

Dance facts

Ten thousand communities

Before Europeans came to Africa, there were perhaps as many as 10,000 different states or groupings of people. In the late 1800s, European countries took control of most of the continent. They divided Africa up into countries that had little to do with the groupings that had existed previously. Each of these groupings had their own **culture**, and this can still be seen in the many different kinds of music and dance found within each African country.

▲ Egungun dancers in Benin, western Africa, do a spinning dance that helps them into a trance. They believe that they can then receive messages from their ancestors.

Throwing insults

In one area of Ghana, there is a festival each year to celebrate the god Ntoa. The festival lasts a whole week. During this time, groups move through the streets using song and dance to insult each other or complain about something. On the last day of the festival, the groups do a final performance, where the leaders and elders of the area are there to hear all the insults and complaints. It gives ordinary people the chance to vent their frustration, and the elders learn what problems are most bothering people.

take the shape of animals or objects, or that could possess a person and speak through them. Many religious dances were repetitive and hypnotic. People danced until they were in a **trance**. They believed that gods or spirits could enter their bodies while they were in a trance.

Amateurs and experts

At ceremonies and celebrations, some dances are open for anyone to join in. Other dances are performed by special dance teams who practice for months before the occasion. Even if only a few people are actually dancing, those watching are still involved. They may sing, clap, and shout out if someone impresses them with extra-skillful moves.

A particular dance may be only one part of a longer event. Some occasions can involve a mixture of many different kinds of dancing.

In the Gelede ceremony in Nigeria, one dancer appears in a large mask and dances in praise of the Earth Mother goddess. There are also other dances involving young boys, older boys, and young men, and after the main ceremony everyone takes part in dancing and singing that goes on all night.

Temples and Courts

In North Africa and Asia, dancing is not as closely connected to social occasions as it is in Africa south of the Sahara. Many Asian dances were originally religious dances performed in temples or dances made to be performed in royal courts.

Temple dances

In the religion called **Hinduism**, dance has always been a part of worshiping god. Shiva (see box) is also known as Lord of the Dance. Many women served as devadasis (servants of god) in **Hindu** temples. The devadasis danced in praise of the god. The best-known style of Indian dance is called bharata natyam. In this style, the dancer tells stories about the gods through dance and complex gestures. Only women dance traditional bharata natyam (see page 38).

▶ The complicated hand gestures of this bharata natyam dancer are known as mudras. The dancer paints the ends of her fingers red, which makes the gestures show more clearly.

Dance facts

Lord of the Dance
In the Hindu religion, there is only one god, Brahman, who can be worshiped in many forms. The three most important forms are Brahma, who created the universe, Vishnu, who maintains the universe, and Shiva, who destroys the universe. Shiva is also sometimes known as Nataraja, or Lord of the Dance.

▲ Not all Indian dance is traditional. Shobana Jeyasingh is Indian but works in the United Kingdom. She uses both bharata natyam and modern dance in her **choreography**. This piece, *Faultline*, is about city life and Asian gang **culture**.

From the 5th century BCE onward, Hinduism and temple dances spread from India to Southeast Asia. In Bali, Indonesia, dances to the gods are still performed in thousands of small temples each year. Each village has three temples: one for Brahma, one for Vishnu, and one for Shiva. Every 210 days, each temple has an Odalan—a "birthday party" for their god. On the Odalan, everyone in the village brings offerings of food and carvings for the gods. The celebrations include music and dancing.

In Central Asia, dances are part of elaborate ceremonies carried out each year in some **Buddhist** monasteries. In one dance, the monks wear rich silk costumes and black hats, so the dance is known as the black hat dance. Some of the dancers have skulls on their hats and wear ugly masks. These represent evil spirits. Other dancers have masks to represent gods. The gods and evil spirits battle until the evil spirits are driven out.

Amazing fact

Ancient handbook
The basic "rule book" for Indian **classical dance** is called the *Natya Sastra*. It was written around 2,000 years ago. It is a handbook explaining everything related to traditional performing arts, including dance, music, drama, costumes, and makeup. According to the *Natya Sastra*, dance was originally created by Lord Brahma. To create the book, he drew on the four Vedas, the oldest holy writings of Hinduism. Brahma then wrote everything down in a book, the *Natya Veda*. He gave this to his son, the sage Bharata. Bharata passed the book on to his 100 sons in the *Natya Sastra*.

▲ Sufi Muslims believe dance is a kind of worship. These Sufis are performing a dervish dance.

Court dances

In the past there have been large empires in China, India, and Southeast Asia. In India the early empires were Hindu or Buddhist, but then in the 16th and 17th centuries the Mughals ruled the area. The Mughals were **Muslims**, and they thought that having dances to worship god was **sacrilege**. The result was that the temple dances changed. Instead of being stories about love of god, they became human love stories and were performed in the courts of Mughal rulers. The dances were more about brilliance and skill than devotion to god.

Amazing fact

Whirling dervishes

In **Islam**, dance is often seen as unsuitable for Muslims. However, in one kind of Islamic worship, known as Sufism, dance plays a central role. Dervish dances are part of Sufi religious ceremonies. Dancers spin with one arm raised to the sky and the other palm down toward the earth. This position symbolizes giving and taking. As the dance continues, the spinning gets faster, and the dancers throw back their heads. Often, they go into a **trance**, which they believe brings them closer to god.

Dancing was also important in the courts of other Asian rulers. In Cambodia, the Angkor empire lasted 600 years, from the 9th to the 15th centuries. During that time, two kinds of glittering court dance developed: lakon nok (unmasked dance) for women, and lakon kawl (masked dance) for men.

Cambodian court dances use gestures similar to those in bharata natyam. Dancers wear elaborate costumes and tall, glittering headdresses.

China was an empire almost continuously for over 2,000 years, from about 200 BCE until 1950. During the T'ang dynasty (618–907), dance was particularly popular in the emperor's court. Emperor Ming Hwang set up the Pear Garden Academy, where performers were trained to act, sing, and perform acrobatics as well as dance. This combination of dance, theater, and music became the basis for Chinese Opera (see page 29).

Court dances were also performed from about 50 BCE at the courts of the Koguryo kingdom, which ruled north Korea and part of China. The kingdom collapsed around 668 CE, but the dances survived in the royal courts of Japan. They became known as bugaku dances. Some bugaku dances have survived in Japan to the present day.

Music and Dance

Dancing is rarely performed without music. In modern Europe and the United States, the music used for dance is often recorded, and the dance and music may be created completely separately. In African and Asian dance, music is traditionally live, and the music and dance are often inseparable. In African dance the dancers sometimes follow changes in the music, then at other times the musicians follow the dancers. In many kinds of Asian dance a story is told, partly through singing and partly through dance and drama. Without both parts the story is not complete.

▼ Percussion instruments such as drums and the balafon (xylophone) are important in many kinds of African music. These musicians are from Burkina in western Africa.

A bundle of rhythms

When you think of African music you probably think of drums. It is true that a few kinds of African music are played by drum ensembles (groups). However, most African music includes other instruments, such as balafons (xylophones), thumb pianos, harps, flutes, horns, shakers, and bells. Singing is also an important part of most African music.

Although drums are not the only instruments in African music, they are important. This is because the rhythm of a piece of music is as important as the tune. There is not just one rhythm—there are lots. Usually there is a basic pulse, a simple pattern played on a sharp-toned instrument such as a cowbell. Other rhythms, played on drums or other instruments, fit together with each other and with the basic pulse, like pieces of a jigsaw puzzle. If there is singing, the tune rides over the top of this complex network of rhythms.

Technique

Following the cues

Agbeko is a war dance of the Anlo-Ewe people of Ghana. The dance is made up of a series of sections, each of which has a distinctive rhythmic pattern.

The change from one dance section to another is controlled by the master drummer—the head of the musicians who play for agbeko. He plays the rhythm of the next section on the master drum as a cue for the dancers that the music is about to change. He then leads the musicians into the music for the next section.

Picking up on the music cues and changing quickly and smoothly into the next section of dance requires a great deal of skill. Dancers practice for several months before an agbeko performance.

Different dances connect with the music in different ways. In some dances, the feet follow the underlying pulse, while gestures and other movements emphasize other rhythms in the dance. In other dances, the dancers perform complex stepping rhythms.

In some dances, there is space for **improvised** (made-up) **solos.** The lead musician or master drummer watches the solo dancer and improvises, too, inspired by the dancer's rhythms.

Tablas and gamelans

There is no common thread to the music used in Asian dance. In some cases, rhythm is very important, as in African dance. Some pieces of Indian **classical dance** involve complex rhythms. In the *nritta*, or "pure dance" sections of kathak dance, the dancers and musicians improvise complex rhythms within a particular time cycle (a certain number of beats). As in African dance, the dancer and the musicians may divide the time cycle up in different ways, so that several different rhythms are happening at the same time.

▶ This kathak dancer is performing at a festival in Khajuraho, India. As in bharata natyam, facial expressions are important. Kathak also involves fast turns and stamping steps in complex rhythms.

Biography

Super-fast feet

Binda Din Maharaj was a great kathak dancer in the early 19th century. He also composed many pieces of kathak music. Binda Din and his brother Kalka Prasad were dancers in the court of Nawab Wajid Ali Shah. At the nawab's court, the two brothers took kathak dancing to new heights. According to one story, when he was just seven years old, Binda Din danced for 12 hours in a contest with the court's top kathak drummer, Kodau Singh. At the end of the contest Binda Din was dancing so fast that his feet were just a blur. Kodau Singh lost track of the dance, and Binda Din won the contest.

In Asian dance music a wider range of instruments are used than in Africa. A music group playing for Indian classical dance, for instance, will include several stringed instruments, such as a sitar (a large, guitar-like stringed instrument) and a sarangi (a bowed string instrument). It will also include tablas (drums) and probably a harmonium. In contrast, Southeast Asian dancers dance to the music of a pipad or a gamelan. The main instruments in these groups are metallophones. These are instruments a little like xylophones, but the notes are made by metal bells instead of metal bars.

▼ These musicians are in a gamelan orchestra in Bali, Indonesia.

In Chinese Opera, dancers act and sing in addition to moving. The music is played by an orchestra of string instruments, wind instruments, drums, and gongs. The orchestra for Japanese **Noh** plays (a mixture of dance, music, and singing) is much simpler—just several drums and a flute. However, there is also a chorus of singers who sing and chant the story of the play.

Styles and Techniques

How do African and Asian dances look? Are they difficult or easy to do? How do the dances compare with Western dance styles such as ballet and ballroom? Let's take a closer look and find out.

Amazing fact

Dancing all night

Kathakali is a kind of dance-drama from Kerala, in southern India. In the past, a group of Kathakali performers would perform together for a king or ruler and his or her court. However, today each Kathakali performer works for himself.

When a performance is put on, the 20 or so performers may meet for the first time on the evening of the performance. They do not know beforehand what stories they will be doing. However, they will manage a performance of 8 or 10 hours without any problems.

Close to the ground

In ballet dancing, the dancers work hard to get away from the ground. When ballerinas dance they seem to float above the ground, and when male ballet dancers perform huge leaps, they seem to hang in the air for a second.

Most African dancing is grounded, rather than light. Dancers move with bent legs, and they stamp or slide their feet, crouch down, and hit the ground with sticks or spears. In some dances there are leaps and acrobatics, but the body still has a sense of weight. This weightiness adds to the sense of excitement when the dancers move fast or leap.

Many Asian dance styles are also grounded. In India's **classical dances** such as bharata natyam and Kathakali (see box), and in the **court** dances of Southeast Asia, the dancers sink into low positions with deep leg bends. There is rarely any jumping.

Not all African and Asian dances are so grounded. In the Maasai jumping dances (see page 9), the dancers skyrocket off the ground and seem to jump impossibly high. In Manipuri (a style of Indian dance), the men do lots of spectacular leaps while playing a small drum slung around their neck.

▲ The pung cholam is a Manipuri dance from Asia. The dancers use their whole bodies to move in an expressive way.

Slippery hips

In most kinds of Western dance, the back stays mostly upright and the body moves as one piece. African dance is very different. In some dances the body is upright, but in others the body leans forward. Dancers move the back and hips in many different ways. In dances from Ghana, for example, the upper back moves constantly, curving and flexing with the rhythm of the music. In other dances from eastern and southern Africa, the hips circle and shake while the upper back is still.

In most Asian dances, gestures of the arms and head are more important than back movements. Gestures and expressions are especially relevant to Indian dance styles. They all have meanings that help illustrate the stories told in the dancing. Similar gestures are used in Southeast Asian dance, but they are decorative rather than meaningful.

Amazing fact

Hands and faces

The *Natya Sastra* (see page 13) includes descriptions of hundreds of gestures and body positions, many of which are used in bharata natyam and Kathakali. There are 6 modes of resting, 5 kinds of leap, and 32 gaits (ways of walking). There are 28 gestures for a single hand and 24 for both hands. Some gestures have as many as 72 different meanings, depending on how they are used. There are also 13 movements for the head, 7 for the eyebrows, 6 for the nose, 6 for the cheek, 7 for the chin, 9 for the neck, and 36 for the eyes!

▲ Kathakali dancers (see page 20) use many of the gestures and expressions in the *Natya Sastra*. This boy is practicing facial expressions.

Beijing Opera dancers learn acrobatics, singing, acting, and other skills such as scarf dancing.

Learning dances

In villages where traditional African dances were originally performed, dancing is something that children still learn from an early age. There are many traditional children's dances, which are simple and easy to learn. There are also dances that are meant specifically for other age groups. Young men learn athletic dances that help keep them fit. Zulu and Ndebele men of South Africa, for instance, learn dances that recall the victories of past warriors. Older men and women perform slower, more stately dances.

Among some African people, dances are particularly difficult and complex. Not everyone can learn them, and doing them well requires practice. For their Adua dance, young Asante women of Ghana train for months before a performance. Other kinds of African dance—for example, some Yoruba dances—need other kinds of skill. Many dances require dancers to **improvise**, meaning the dancers must be able to make up new movements on the spot.

In contrast with African dance, classical Asian dances usually involve a great deal of training. For dance forms such as Kathakali or Chinese Opera, children begin training in special schools at an early age. For Chinese Opera, children have to train in dancing, singing, and acting. They also learn acrobatics and martial arts for the many battle scenes.

Telling Stories

Do you like musicals? Have you ever seen *Grease* or *The Lion King*? A musical combines drama with dancing and music to tell a story. In many African and Asian **cultures**, dance, music, and drama are combined in a similar way. The performers are telling a story, and they use dancing, acting, singing, music, and even acrobatics or martial arts to do it.

Social drama

African dances rarely tell actual stories, but they are often dramatic. Dances can be used to praise leaders, insult rivals, or to express religious beliefs. The Akan people of Ghana use gestures, which have meaning, in their dances. Reaching upward with one or both hands, for example, means, "I look to God," and putting one finger under the right eye means, "I have no opinion: I will see how things work out."

Religious dances are among the most dramatic of African dances. To understand these dances, we need to know a little about the religion involved. The Yoruba people of Nigeria believe that when they die they go to Orun (Paradise or Heaven), where they live with

Dance facts

Contante (Happiness)

Today, African dancers may not perform in traditional settings, but they may still use traditional steps and stories. Contante is a dance made by the *djeli* (musician and storyteller) Kunda Kouyate. The dance is based on a Senegalese legend of a young boy named Songalo. Both Songalo's parents died, and he was so sad that he would not eat, talk, or play. The village king called upon the *griots* (musicians and dancers) to bring Songalo happiness. The *griots* told the boy his family history, and how good his parents and other ancestors were. They reassured him that the people of the village would look after him well. The stories and songs made Songalo feel better. To celebrate, the king called for a big party.

▲ Egungun dancers wear scarves and masks to hide their normal identity. This makes it easier for them to take on the identity of an ancestor.

god and the spirits. For a time after they die, spirits can communicate with god, but also with their relatives on Earth. In this way, a family's **ancestors** can talk to the living members of the family.

One way that the living can communicate with their ancestors is through special dancers, known as the Egungun. The Egungun wear masks and long cloaks or **raffia** coverings. When an Egungun dances and sings or speaks, the voice of an ancestor or group of ancestors speaks through him. Every year there is an Egungun festival, when the Egungun go to family graves and houses, stopping every so often to dance. They bless the living members of a family on behalf of their ancestors.

Some Egungun dancers perform for entertainment rather than for religious reasons. Their dances are about events that have taken place in the community. They might mimic people such as tourists and poke fun at them. Their dances are like short stories or sketches.

Gods, kings, and snake spirits

In Asia, many kinds of dance are concerned with storytelling. Indian **classical dances**, dance dramas from Thailand and Indonesia, Chinese Opera, and Kabuki theater are all storytelling dances. In India and Southeast Asia, many of the stories are from the two epic **Hindu** stories, the Mahabharata and the Ramayana. The Mahabharata is the story of a feud between two families that turns into a long, drawn-out war, in which the god Krishna becomes involved. The Ramayana tells the story of Rama, an Indian prince who is also an **incarnation** of the god Vishnu. Rama and his wife Sita are exiled to the forest, and Sita is captured by the evil demon Ravana. After many adventures, Rama rescues Sita, with much help from the powerful monkey-king Hanuman. Eventually, Rama and Sita return to their home city, and Rama is crowned king.

▲ Kathakali dancers act out a story from the epic Indian story *The Mahabharata.*

These stories are told in many different ways in different cultures. In Kathakali, the actors speak only with movements and gestures. A singer helps to tell the story through a song, accompanied by musicians.

The Thai version of the Ramayana is called the Ramakien. Children train from a young age to learn the dance styles for the Ramakien. Some train as demons or monkeys, while others become heroes. The demons and monkeys learn martial arts, acrobatics, and aggressive movements to illustrate fights. The heroes move more slowly and lightly and make elaborate gestures with their hands and fingers.

In Cambodian nang shek and Indonesian wayang kulit theater, the stories are told through puppets. This is not really dance, but in Java, Indonesia, the puppet plays of wayang kulit have been adapted for human dancers. The dance follows the same structure as the puppet plays, and in places the dancers even mimic the stiff movements of the puppets.

Dances from Japan and Korea tell different stories. Japanese Kabuki stories are extremely varied. Some tell stories of adventure—for instance, the story of the 47 Ronin (loyal servants) who track down their lord's killer and take revenge. Other stories are about love or lost love. Many of the stories have sad or tragic endings.

Biography

Okuni

Today, Japanese Kabuki theater is traditionally performed by men. However, Kabuki was first invented by a woman, called Okuni of Izumo. Okuni was probably originally a temple dancer in Izumo, but she moved to Kyoto. Her dancing was much livelier than the dances in **Noh** theater, which was popular at the time. Soon Okuni had a whole troupe of women dancers, and they were popular with the samurai (lords) and the Shogun (ruler). This was the first Kabuki company.

Later in the 17th century women and young boys were banned from performing, and Kabuki became an all-male art. However, in recent years women have once again begun to perform Kabuki.

▲ The acrobatics and impressive theatrical effects make Beijing Opera popular in theaters around the world.

The most common story in Chinese Opera is a **Buddhist** tale called *Journey to the West*. It is the story of how the monk Tripitaka journeys west to India to collect the Buddhist scriptures and takes them back to China. To protect him on his journey, Tripitaka has three companions—Pigsy, Sandy, and Monkey. Monkey is the main character in the stories. He is always up to mischief, but he also protects Tripitaka from many dangers and in the end is rewarded by the Buddha himself.

Biography

Chinese Opera star

The movie star Jackie Chan has made a string of successful films that combine martial arts with comedy. His movies always include impressive stunts and acrobatics, too. Jackie learned most of his martial arts and acrobatic skills in the China Drama Academy in Hong Kong. He trained there for ten years, from the age of seven. At the time Chinese Opera was not very popular in Hong Kong, so Master Yu, who was in charge of the school, got work for some of his students in movies. Soon Jackie was working as a stuntman. He went on to act in kung fu films, and eventually made his own movies.

▼ Movie star Jackie Chan began his acting career in Bejing Opera.

Masks, Costumes, and Makeup

For many kinds of African dance, costumes and props are an important part of the performance. Some dances look truly spectacular, with dancers on stilts or wearing enormous masks. Asian **classical dance** can be spectacular, too, as it almost always involves elaborate costumes and makeup.

Masquerades

A masquerade is a masked dance. Masquerades are found across Africa and Asia. The masks can be small or large and can serve different purposes. In the funeral dances of the Dogon people of Mali, each dancer wears a different mask. With their masks on, the dancers become spirits that lead the dead person into the spirit world. The most important mask of the dance is the *iminana* or "mother" mask. It is huge—it can be 15 feet (4.5 meters) tall. Other masks are of animals, protector spirits, and even foods that the dead person can take into the spirit world.

Other African masks transform the dancers into animals. The Bambara people of Mali carry masks carved in the shape of antelopes and other wild animals. The dancers imitate the movements of the animals in a dance to renew the fertility of the land.

Amazing fact

Fire dancers
The Bainings Fire Dance is a masked dance from Papua New Guinea. The dancers take the names of recently dead people and wear huge masks. They dance around a large fire before plunging into it, running through the flames. Because the dancers have taken the names of dead spirits, they believe they are protected from the fire.

There are many masked dances in Asia, too. In the wayang topeng dances of Thailand, Burma, and Cambodia, the men wear masks. In the Tibetan black hat dance (see page 13), dancers wear masks representing dead people, evil spirits, and the spirits of great teachers of the past. There is also a clown who wears a mask with a silly face.

The Chinese lion dance is a masquerade that happens at New Year. Two people dress up as a lion, one being the front legs and head, the other the back legs. The eyes and mouth of the lion's head are movable.

▶ This is a Balinese topeng performer. Topeng is masked dance-drama. Topeng performances tell historical stories or are part of religious celebrations.

Makeup and costumes

If dancers do not wear masks, they often have elaborate makeup instead. African dancers sometimes use white makeup or body painting. In Kathakali, Japanese Kabuki, and Beijing Opera, the makeup helps the audience to understand the nature of the characters on stage. In Kathakali, different characters have different colors of makeup. *Paccha* (green) characters are kings, heroes, or god-like characters. *Katti*, or knife characters, are also mostly green, but have a red "knife" mark on each cheek. These characters are brave, but also arrogant and evil. Red indicates vicious and horrible characters, while black makeup indicates wild hunters and forest-dwellers. *Minukku* (radiant) characters are gentle and spiritual. They wear much simpler makeup that is mostly yellow.

Kathakali dancers also wear elaborate costumes. Their enormous skirts are made from nearly 56 feet (17 meters) of cloth, and many characters have tall, richly decorated headdresses. Southeast Asian **court** dancers are, if anything, even more extravagantly dressed. Their jackets have upturned shoulders, and their wide, knee-length pants are covered with gold thread and intricate decoration.

Dance facts

Making up

In Kathakali, makeup for even the most minor character has to be applied by skilled makeup artists, and it takes several hours. Actors lie on the floor while they are being made up and often take the opportunity to catch up on their sleep! Just before going on stage, Kathakali actors place a small seed in each eye, which turns the whites of the eyes red. Eye movements are an important part of Kathakali acting, and making them red adds to the dramatic effect.

▲ A makeup artist adds the finishing touches to the makeup of the character Hanuman, the monkey-god.

▲ The Dogon people of Mali perform elaborate funeral dances when someone dies. Some of the dancers perform on stilts.

Some African dancers also wear elaborate costumes. Egungun dancers (see page 25) wear fantastic costumes made up of many different colored pieces of cloth. They often wear body decorations rather than full costumes. Many dancers have headdresses or other costumes made from feathers. **Raffia** is also a popular material for costumes, because it is light and airy and allows the dancer to move freely. Dancers on stilts appear in some dances and ceremonies. Dogon funeral ceremonies, for example, involve stilt dancers. The Makonde or Makua dancers from Kenya and Mozambique also dance on stilts, as do some dancers from Guinea.

Amazing fact

Quick-change specialists
In Kabuki theater, sudden, startling set and costume changes often happen in view of the audience. Many Kabuki costumes are layered, and an actor can change completely by removing one layer. Often stage assistants, dressed completely in black, help with these sudden transformations.

Spreading the Influence

In different ways, dance from Africa and Asia has spread around the globe. African dance began to spread in the 15th century, when European traders began buying people from west and central Africa and selling them in the Americas as slaves.

Mixing traditions

Most of the slaves who were sent to the Americas worked on plantations (large farms) in the southern United States, the Caribbean, and parts of South America. They took African dance and music traditions with them. The slaves came from many different parts of Africa, and different groups of slaves had different traditions of music and dance. In the Americas the different traditions were eventually combined, along with ideas from white, European-style dance and music. The result was completely new kinds of dance and music.

▶ This is a lindy hop competition in New York. Lindy hop is a U.S. dance that mixes European and African dance styles.

While black people were kept as slaves, their dances and music did not spread much beyond the plantations. However, once slavery ended in the 19th century, some of these African/European dances became popular with white people. One of the first popular dances that was clearly African-influenced was the lindy hop. Lindy hopping was danced to jazz music. It began at the Savoy Ballroom in Harlem, in New York City. Lindy hop was a partner dance, like European ballroom dances such as the waltz or the foxtrot. However, it was much more exciting than a waltz. The partners did not always dance together—they spent part of their time **improvising** elaborate dance steps.

In South America, dances such as the samba from Brazil and the rumba from Cuba were strongly influenced by Africa. In both Cuba and Brazil, the link with African dance was stronger than in the United States. This was because in both places, many of the slaves came from a single area, so all the slaves had the same dances, music, and religion. In Cuba, most of the slaves were Yoruba people from Nigeria. In Brazil, they were from Congo and Angola. Samba dancing, and the original style of Cuban rumba, were both very similar to African dance styles.

In the 1940s and 1950s, African-American dancers Katherine Dunham and Pearl Primus traveled to the Caribbean and to West Africa to learn about African and African-American dancing. They used ideas and movements from what they learned in their own modern dance performances. Alvin Ailey, one of the great modern dancers of the 1960s and 1970s, was also interested in African and African-American dance styles.

There are African influences in many other American dance styles, such as jazz dance, tap, salsa, and even hip-hop dance. Hip-hop has traveled back across the Atlantic and is as popular in Africa as it is in the United States.

Technique

African characteristics

How can we tell that a dance style has African connections? Sometimes we only know from looking at the history of a dance that it has connections with Africa. However, there are also some things that are common in African-style dances. The hips and back are much freer than in European-style dances, and the body is grounded. It often features high-speed footwork, too.

Technique

African-style religious ceremonies
In parts of the Caribbean and South America, African-style religious ceremonies have survived from the time of slavery and still take place today. As in African ceremonies such as the Yoruba Gelede dance and Egungun ceremonies (see pages 11 and 25), the musicians begin with a slow, hypnotic drumbeat and gradually play faster and faster. The dancers follow the music in dances that often involve spinning and repeated movements. At the height of the ceremony some dancers go into a **trance**, and their **ancestors** or other spirits speak through them. Santeria from Cuba, Candomblé from Brazil, and vodun (voodoo) from Haiti are all African-style religions of this kind.

▲ This young girl is at an Umbanda ceremony in Brazil. Umbanda is a religion similar to Candomblé and Santeria.

▲ Bollywood star Rani Mukerji dances in the movie *Bunty aur Babli*, about a pair of likable crooks. Bollywood dance styles draw on traditional Indian dances such as kathak and bhangra.

Dance in the movies

Today, many countries in Asia have dance troupes that tour internationally and perform their traditional dances. Bharata natyam, kathak, Kathakali, and Japanese Kabuki dances have all become known outside Asia in this way. However, relatively few people go to theaters, and most people never see these performances. The main way that people in other countries see Asian dancing is through movies.

Bollywood movies are films made mainly in the Hindi language in Mumbai, India. In most Bollywood movies, romance, adventure, comedy, dance, and music are all mixed together in a three-hour epic. In older Bollywood movies, the dancing is based on Indian traditional and **folk dances**, usually kathak and bhangra. In modern Bollywood movies the dancing is a mixture of traditional and more modern Western styles.

Technique

Bhangra beat

Bhangra is a folk dance from the Punjab, in South Asia. Originally it was danced to celebrate the end of harvest, but it later became a general celebration dance, performed at birthday parties, weddings, and all kinds of social occasions. In the 1980s, a new kind of bhangra called freestyle appeared, in which the dancers could improvise. Bhangra music gets its distinctive sound from a two-headed drum called a dhol, which has a high sound on one end and a low sound on the other. Today, Asian musicians combine bhangra sounds with hip-hop, reggae, and other modern sounds, and bhangra dancing is part of many Bollywood movies.

Changing Styles

African and Asian countries have changed greatly in the last hundred years or so, and dance has changed, too. In both Africa and Asia, many people have moved from the country to the city. In the cities people from different **cultures** mix together, and often the distinct dance styles of particular places are lost. Better communications mean that people in places as remote as Tibet come into contact with Western-style dance and music, via movies, television, and the Internet.

The tourist trade

In the 19th century, many kinds of Asian and African dance almost disappeared, but more recently traditional dance styles have been revived. Traditional dances in Africa and Asia are popular for two main reasons. First, as Western culture has spread to other countries, people have tried to preserve the traditional dances of their own country or area so that their culture is not lost. Second, tourists visiting an African or Asian country are often interested in seeing the dances of that country. Many "traditional" dance troupes have been formed to perform for tourists.

Biography

19th-century spin-doctors
Indian **classical dance** is thriving today, but in the 19th century it almost completely died out. Temple dancing, or Desiattam, had a bad reputation, and the women who danced it (devadasis) were looked down on. However, in the late 19th century four brothers, Chinniyah, Punniah, Vadivelu, and Shivanandam, restored the richness of the original dance style by studying the *Natya Sastra* (see page 13) and temple carvings, and combining these studies with the dances of the devadasis. More people became interested in Desiattam, but it was still not fully accepted. Then in 1932 the Madras Music Academy changed the name of the dance style from Desiattam to bharata natyam. With the change in name, Desiattam's bad reputation was forgotten.

Many traditional dances have had to change in order to survive as tourist attractions. Dances that are not visually exciting do not get performed at all, while other dances are changed for tourists' tastes. Often they are made much shorter. A Kathakali or Kabuki performance that would in the past have gone on all night is cut down to one or two hours. Many African dances were once made for a particular celebration or ritual or to be performed in a particular place. Today, these dances have lost their social importance and are performed for entertainment. An African dance group performing traditional dances today might perform parts of a Yoruba **"coming of age"** dance, a Zulu warrior dance, and a Dogon funeral dance, all in one evening.

The circus-style extravaganza *Afrika! Afrika!* showcases the best in African dance and music.

Updating traditions

Although some kinds of traditional dance are preserved for tourists, other dance traditions are still alive and changing. Some modern Japanese writers continue to write Kabuki plays, and Kabuki performers have also taken Western plays such as Shakespeare's *King Lear* and made Kabuki versions of them. In recent years, women have also begun performing in Kabuki troupes again, for the first time since the 17th century.

Another place where traditional dances have been updated is in the Indonesian island of Bali. Bali is a small island with an incredibly rich dance culture. It has thousands of dance groups. The dances are very popular with tourists who come to Bali. The tourists pay to see performances of these and other dances, both in theaters and also in villages and temples.

In the 1970s, the people of Bali became worried that their sacred dances were losing their sacred character because so many tourists were paying dancers to perform them. So, the Balinese decided that some dances were sacred and could not be danced for money, while for other dances the performers could charge a fee. This has helped to preserve dance traditions without losing the purpose of the sacred dances.

Biography

Super Mario

Balinese dances have always been danced to gamelan music. In the early 20th century, a new kind of gamelan music developed in northern Bali. The new gamelan, known as Kebyar, produced a more brilliant, high-pitched, shimmering sound than the traditional gamelan.

In 1925 a talented young dancer, I Nyoman Mario, created the first new dance for the Kebyar gamelan. He called the dance Kebyar Duduk, which means "sitting Kebyar," because in the middle of the dance there is a long section where the dancers bounce in a squatting position. Mario created a second Kebyar dance piece in 1952: a duet for a man and a woman.

▲ Akram Khan (left) is trained in both kathak and modern dance. He has also worked with dancers in other styles, such as the Dutch dancer Sidi Larbi Cherkaoui.

New dances

Over the last hundred years or so, some completely new kinds of African and Asian dance have developed. In Africa many of the changes in dance were linked to changes that were happening in African music. In African cities, musicians were combining African music ideas with European instruments and music from the United States, such as jazz and blues. Music styles such as Highlife in Nigeria and Ghana, and Congolese rumba in central Africa, were designed to be played in clubs and dance halls.

Many African dancers now train in Western techniques such as modern dance and ballet. Senegalese–French dancer Germaine Acogny, for example, uses both African and modern dance techniques in her **choreography.** In the Americas and Europe, there are many African and Afro-Caribbean dance groups that perform some traditional dances but also make their own dance pieces and dance dramas.

Asian dancers have also drawn on Western dance ideas to develop their own dance styles. In Japan in the late 1950s and early 1960s, dancer Tatsumi Hijikata developed a new style of dance called Ankoku Butoh (now usually called just "butoh"). Hijikata was trained in a German style of modern dance, but he also drew on Japanese traditions to create butoh as a truly modern Japanese style. More recently other Asian dancers have modernized traditional dances or mixed them with other styles. The Cloud Gate Dance Theater of Taiwan, for example, uses Tai Chi, meditation, martial arts, Chinese Opera movement, modern dance, and ballet in its dancing.

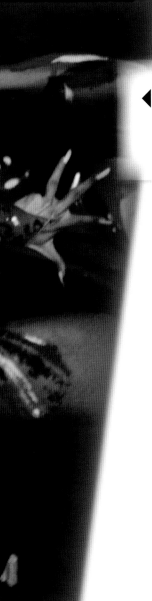

Yang Liping is a dancer from Yunnan province in China. She has created her own style of dance that includes some elements of traditional **folk** styles but also draws on European dance and theater.

Many dancers working abroad have created their own styles that mix Asian and Western styles. Dancers in the United States such as Pandit Chitresh Das and Jason Samuels Smith have explored the connections between kathak and tap dancing, while in the United Kingdom Shobana Jeyasingh and Akram Khan mix Indian styles with modern dance.

Today, more and more dancers are interested in combining traditions or crossing boundaries between dance styles. However, there are also people working to keep alive the traditional dances of Africa and Asia. It is important to keep this combination of preserving traditional dances and creating new ones. This is the best way to keep alive the tremendous variety and richness of African and Asian dance.

Amazing fact

Monkey: Journey to the West
Damon Albarn, writer and singer for the rock group Gorillaz, and Jamie Hewlett, who draws the Gorillaz characters, teamed up with Chinese-American director Chen Shi-Zheng to make a new version of the Chinese Opera classic *Journey to the West* (see page 29). This theater production combined Chinese Opera with animated cartoons drawn by Jamie Hewlett and electronic music from Damon Albarn. The performance toured Europe in 2007.

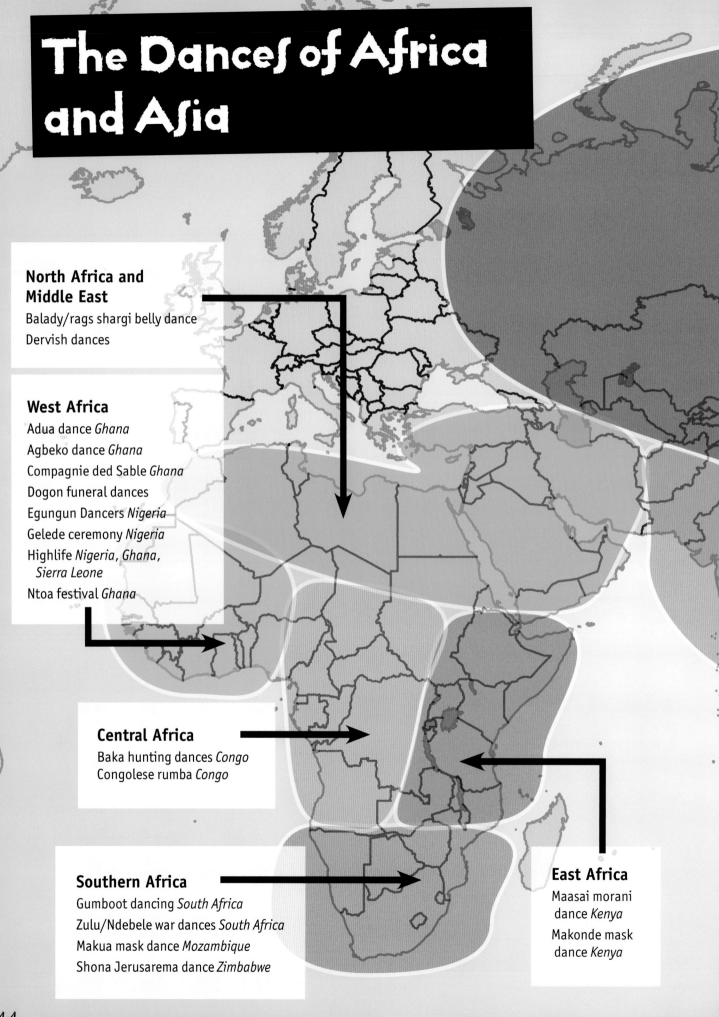

The Dances of Africa and Asia

North Africa and Middle East
Balady/raqs shargi belly dance
Dervish dances

West Africa
Adua dance *Ghana*
Agbeko dance *Ghana*
Compagnie ded Sable *Ghana*
Dogon funeral dances
Egungun Dancers *Nigeria*
Gelede ceremony *Nigeria*
Highlife *Nigeria, Ghana, Sierra Leone*
Ntoa festival *Ghana*

Central Africa
Baka hunting dances *Congo*
Congolese rumba *Congo*

Southern Africa
Gumboot dancing *South Africa*
Zulu/Ndebele war dances *South Africa*
Makua mask dance *Mozambique*
Shona Jerusarema dance *Zimbabwe*

East Africa
Maasai morani dance *Kenya*
Makonde mask dance *Kenya*

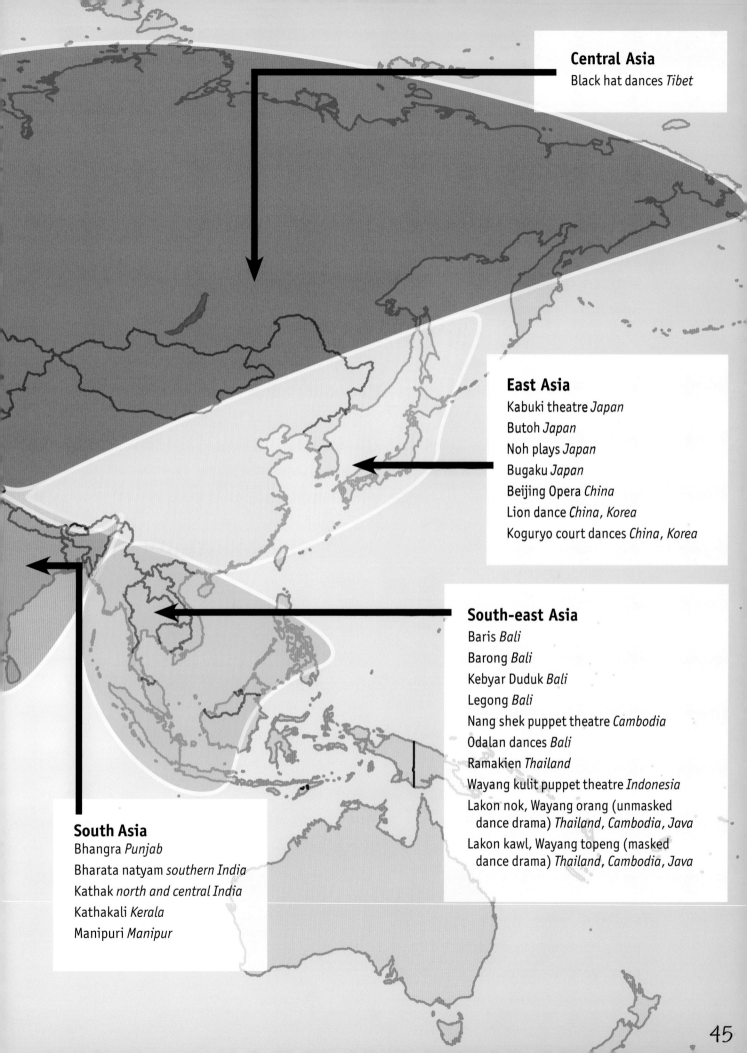

Central Asia
Black hat dances *Tibet*

East Asia
Kabuki theatre *Japan*
Butoh *Japan*
Noh plays *Japan*
Bugaku *Japan*
Beijing Opera *China*
Lion dance *China, Korea*
Koguryo court dances *China, Korea*

South-east Asia
Baris *Bali*
Barong *Bali*
Kebyar Duduk *Bali*
Legong *Bali*
Nang shek puppet theatre *Cambodia*
Odalan dances *Bali*
Ramakien *Thailand*
Wayang kulit puppet theatre *Indonesia*
Lakon nok, Wayang orang (unmasked
   dance drama) *Thailand, Cambodia, Java*
Lakon kawl, Wayang topeng (masked
   dance drama) *Thailand, Cambodia, Java*

South Asia
Bhangra *Punjab*
Bharata natyam *southern India*
Kathak *north and central India*
Kathakali *Kerala*
Manipuri *Manipur*

45

Glossary

ancestor relative who lived long ago

Buddhist follower of Buddhism, or something related to Buddhism, a religion founded in India by Siddhartha Gautama, or Buddha. Buddhists believe that we are reborn again and again until we reach nirvana (happiness).

choreography making dances

classical dance any dance style that developed in the past over many years and now has a fairly fixed, complex technique. Dancers usually need to start young and train hard to properly learn a classical dance style.

"coming of age" period of time when a child develops into an adult

culture way a group of people lives— the language(s), beliefs, customs, and traditions they share

folk dance dance that is made for ordinary people to do together, rather than for performing

Hindu follower of Hinduism, or something related to Hinduism

Hinduism religion that originated in India. Hinduism is very varied, and Hindus worship many gods, but all of them are aspects of the great god, Brahman.

improvise make things up on the spot

incarnation particular human form of a god

Islam Middle Eastern religion based on following the one god, Allah, and the teachings of the prophet Mohammed

kimono long, loose robe with wide sleeves, tied at the waist with a broad sash

Muslim follower of Islam

Noh kind of Japanese theater in which the actors move but do not speak, while the musicians sing, speak, or chant the story and the words of the characters

ocher dye that can be a range of colors, from yellow to red to brown

raffia fibrous material obtained from the raffia palm tree

sacrilege something that is against the basic beliefs or values of a religion

solo dance performed by one person

trance half-conscious, hypnotized state of mind

Further Information

Books

Asante, Kariamu Welsh. *African Dance (World of Dance)*. New York: Chelsea House, 2004.

Bingham, Jane. *African Art and Culture (World Art & Culture)*. Chicago: Raintree, 2004.

Descutner, Janet. *Asian Dance (World of Dance)*. New York: Chelsea House, 2004.

Gutierrez, Peter. *Eastern Asia (World of Music)*. Chicago: Heinemann Library, 2008.

Khanduri, Kamini. *Western Asia (World of Music)*. Chicago: Heinemann Library, 2008.

Solway, Andrew. *Africa (World of Music)*. Chicago: Heinemann Library, 2008.

Websites

YouTube is a good place to find video clips of many of the dance styles in the book. You can find specific information and images at the following sites.

www.artsalive.ca/en/dan/dance101/forms.asp#afro-caribbean

A brief introduction to 40 different dance forms, including many from Africa and Asia.

www.artindia.net/index1.html

Lots of information about Indian classical and folk dance.

http://xroads.virginia.edu/~ug03/lucas/dancehome.html

The story of the cakewalk and the lindy hop.

www.mama.org/masks/index.htm

Examples of some African dance masks from the Museum of Ancient and Modern Art in Penn Valley, California.

www.pbs.org/wnet/freetodance/index.html

The story of African-American dance in the United States.

www.worldartswest.org/plm/

Every year there is an ethnic dance festival in San Francisco. "People Like Me" is a guide to the kinds of music and dance in the festival.

Index

acrobatics 20, 22, 23, 24, 27, 29
African dances 4, 6, 7, 8–11, 16, 17, 20, 21, 23, 24–25, 30, 32, 33, 34–35, 38, 39, 41
Afro-American dancing 34, 35, 36
agbeko 17
ancestors, communicating with 9, 24, 25, 36
Asian dances 5, 6–7, 12–15, 16, 18–19, 20, 21–22, 23, 26–29, 30, 31, 32, 33, 37, 38, 40, 41, 42–43

Bali 7, 13, 19, 31, 40
ballet 20, 41, 42
baris 7
Beijing Opera 6, 7, 15, 19, 23, 26, 28, 29, 32, 42, 43
Benin 10
bhangra 37
bharata natyam 12, 13, 20, 22, 37, 38
Binda Din Maharaj 18
black hat dance 13, 31
Bollywood 5, 37
Buddhism 13, 28
bugaku dances 15
butoh 42

Cambodia 15, 27, 31
celebrations 10, 11, 13, 37, 39
ceremonial dances 4, 8, 9, 11, 13, 36, 39
Chan, Jackie 29
children's dances 23
China 6, 7, 15, 23, 28–29, 31
choreographers 7, 13, 35, 40, 41–43
classical dance 13, 18, 19, 20, 23, 26, 30, 38
contante 25
costumes 4, 15, 24, 30, 32-3
court dances 6, 7, 10, 12, 14–15, 20, 32

Dogon dancers 4, 9, 30, 33, 39

Egungun dancers 10, 24, 25, 33, 36

festival dances 5, 11, 24
fire dancers 30
folk dances 6, 37
funeral dances 4, 8, 9, 30, 33, 39

gamelan 19, 40
gestures and expressions 12, 15, 17, 18, 21, 22, 24, 27

Ghana 11, 17, 21, 23, 24, 41
gumboot dancing 8

Hinduism 12, 13, 26
hip hop 5, 35, 37

improvisation 17, 23, 35
India 5, 6, 7, 12-13, 14, 18, 19, 20, 21, 26, 37, 38
Indonesia 13, 19, 26, 27

Japan 5, 7, 15, 19, 27, 40, 42
Java 27
jazz 5, 35, 41
jumping dances 9, 20

Kabuki 5, 26, 27, 32, 33, 37, 39, 40
kathak dance 7, 18, 37, 43
Kathakali 20, 22, 23, 27, 32, 37, 39
Kenya 33
Korea 7, 15, 27

lindy hop 34, 35
lion dance 31

Maasai 9, 20
makeup 30, 32
Mali 4, 30, 33
Manipuri 20
martial arts 23, 24, 27, 29, 42
masks 4, 11, 13, 15, 24, 25, 30–31
masquerades 30
Mozambique 33
music 7, 16–19, 40, 41
    African 16, 17
    Asian 16, 18–19

nang shek 27
Nigeria 11, 24, 41
Noh theater 19, 27

Papua New Guinea 30
percussion 4, 7, 16, 17, 19, 37
puppetry 27

Ramakien 27
religious dances 6, 10–11, 12, 14, 24, 36
rhythms 4, 6, 7, 17, 18, 21
    stepping rhythms 17, 18
rumba 35, 41

salsa 5, 35
samba 5, 35
slavery 34–35
solo dancers 4, 7, 17
spinning dances 10, 14, 36
stilt dancers 30, 33
storytelling 12, 24–27
styles and techniques 20–23
    African 20, 21, 23, 35
    Asian 20, 21–22, 23
Sufism 14

Taiwan 6, 42
tap dancing 35, 43
temple dances 6, 7, 12, 13, 14, 38
Thailand 26, 27, 31
topeng 31
tourist attractions 38, 39, 40
training 15, 23, 27
trances 11, 14, 36

war dances 7, 17
warrior dances 9, 23, 39
wayang kulit 27
whirling dervishes 14

Yoruba dances 23, 24, 36, 39